WHAT WOULD HAPPEN IF...

THE ICE CAPS MELTED?

Written by Claudia Martin

Illustrated by Paula Bossio

WORLD BOOK

www.worldbook.com

READING TIPS

This book asks readers to ponder the question *what would happen if the ice caps melted?* Readers will discover why Earth's ice caps are melting and will consider the major problems that would happen if they melted completely, as well as what we can do to halt the melt. Use these tips to help readers consider the ripple effects of certain actions and events.

Before Reading

Explain to readers that this book uses cause and effect to show how a change in one part of the world can affect the environments and living things throughout the rest of the world. Cause and effect can help us think about why things happen the way they do. It can also help us think about what might happen in the future because of our actions today. Encourage readers to be on the lookout for examples of a cause and effect structure as they explore what would happen if the icecaps melted.

During Reading

Discuss with readers how some actions and events have multiple causes and others have multiple effects. Explain that it can be tricky to keep all the if/then scenarios straight in our minds, so it can be helpful to create a visual guide. Encourage readers to draw and add notes to their own cause and effect maps like those found on pages 10-11, 18-19, 24-25, and 32-33.

After Reading

After finishing the book, discuss with readers how their understandings and opinions of global warming, climate change, and the melting of the polar ice caps have changed. Additionally, you can have readers respond to the comprehension questions included on page 46 and can complete the Chain of Events activity on page 47 to further extend the learning.

Visit **www.worldbook.com/resources** for additional, free educational materials.

*There is a glossary of terms on pages 44–45. Terms defined in the glossary are in boldface type that **looks like this** on their first appearance on any spread (two facing pages).*

Contents

Ice at risk? 4

Getting hotter 6

Precious ice 12

Meltdown! 20

Halt the melt 34

Conclusion 40

Summary 42

Glossary 44

Review and reflect 46

Ice at risk?

Our planet's **poles** are covered by thick, glistening layers of ice, called **ice caps.** Ice also cloaks the peaks of Earth's highest mountains. But our planet is getting warmer, year by year! What would happen if this warmth made the ice caps melt?

You've probably heard people mention **global warming!** They're talking about the rising temperature of Earth's air and oceans. The warming is caused mostly by human activities, including the ways we travel and build. Global warming is causing **climate change. Climate** is the usual weather in a region. So climate change is changes to our weather and seasons.

Did you know that global warming has already shrunk Earth's ice caps? Many people are worried about how this affects the animals, plants—and humans—who live on and around ice caps. Another issue is that the melted ice is trickling into oceans, making **sea levels** rise.

Oof! It's hot out here!

Between dives in search of crabs and snails, a group of walruses rests on the ice that covers the Arctic Ocean.

What would happen if the ice caps start to melt even faster? That could affect not only the animals and people who live nearby—but all of us, all around the world! Could the ice caps melt completely? Read on to find out more.

DID YOU KNOW?

- The South Pole is in the middle of the continent of **Antarctica**.
- The North Pole is in the middle of the **Arctic** Ocean.
- Antarctica has an area of 5.5 million sq miles (14.2 million sq km).
- The Arctic Ocean is covered by up to 5.8 million sq miles (14.9 million sq km) of ice.
- Around 98 percent of Antarctica is covered by ice up to 3 miles (4.9 km) thick.

THINK ABOUT IT!

Do you think weather is important? Can you think of any ways the weather affects your life? For example, have you ever stayed home because of rain, snow, or storms?

Getting hotter

The **ice caps** are shrinking because Earth is getting hotter! In this chapter, let's take a look at why our beautiful planet is warming up. And how much hotter has it gotten?

Let's start by looking back in time! Did you know that Earth's **climate** has changed a lot over the 4.5 billion years since our planet formed? For example, around 100 million years ago, when the awesome dinosaurs were alive, temperatures were 9 to 18 °F (5 to 10 °C) hotter than today. Around 20,000 years ago, Earth had a very cold period—called an ice age—when it was 9 °F (5 °C) colder than it is now.

The dinosaur *Cryolophosaurus* lived on **Antarctica** when Earth was so warm that there was no ice at the **poles**. This meant that there was more liquid, flowing water, so **sea levels** were 165 to 330 ft (50 to 100 m) higher than now.

What's ice?

These long-ago changes in Earth's climate usually happened slowly, over thousands or millions of years. What caused them? It was gradual changes in the sun, in Earth's journey around the sun, and in the blanket of gases that surrounds Earth, known as its **atmosphere.**

Now here's the problem! Today's **global warming** is happening much faster. That's giving humans, other animals, and plants hardly any time to adapt. The main cause of today's global warming is changes in Earth's atmosphere since the end of the 1800's. This was when humans started to burn lots of **fossil fuels** in factories, vehicles, and homes.

Around 20,000 years ago, it was so cold that ice covered a quarter of Earth's land. With so much less liquid water, sea levels were around 410 ft (125 m) below today.

THINK ABOUT IT!

Woolly mammoths were relatives of elephants that had thick fur to keep them warm during the last ice age. They became **extinct** as Earth got hotter. Do you think any of today's furry animals will be affected by global warming?

DID YOU KNOW?

Today, Earth's average surface temperature is 58.6 °F (14.8 °C), which is around 1.9 °F (1 °C) hotter than in 1880.

Let's get a grip on the science! The big cause of **global warming** is the **greenhouse effect**. This is how gases in Earth's **atmosphere** trap the sun's heat—a little like the glass of a greenhouse traps heat! The gases with this warming effect are called **greenhouse gases**. They include **carbon dioxide, methane,** and **nitrous oxide**.

DID YOU KNOW?
Every year, the world burns more than 4,000 times the amount of **fossil fuels** that were burnt in 1776, releasing over 40 billion tons (37 billion metric tons) of carbon dioxide.

Sunlight

Greenhouse gases

Sunlight warms Earth during the day, then at night the planet cools, releasing heat back into the air. Some of the heat is trapped by greenhouse gases.

There's nothing new about greenhouse gases! They're found naturally in Earth's atmosphere. In fact, Earth needs the greenhouse effect to be suitable for life, since, without it, the planet's average surface temperature would be -0.4 °F (-18 °C). That's cold! But since the late 1800's, humans have released too much greenhouse gas into the atmosphere, making the planet warm more quickly than it has for millions of years.

The main cause of these extra greenhouse gases is fossil fuels: coal, oil, and natural gas. These fuels release carbon dioxide when they're burned. Across the world, fossil fuels are burned to make heat, which is used to cook, to warm homes, and to power factory machines and vehicle engines.

GETTING HOTTER

Coal, oil, and gas formed underground from long-dead plants and animals. Fossils of dinosaurs formed in a similar way—but they're much more fun.

Coal

Oil

Natural gas

Hi! My name is Syukuro Manabe and I'm a Japanese American **climate** scientist. In the 1960's, I began to study how **emissions** of greenhouse gases were making the atmosphere hotter. I was one of the first scientists to alert the world to global warming.

THINK ABOUT IT!

When people built the first fossil fuel-powered factories, they didn't know what effect they would have on the planet. If they had known, do you think they would have stopped?

Fossil fuels are not the only cause of **global warming**! Let's take a look at all the main human activities that are warming our planet—and shrinking our slippery **ice caps**.

Deforestation

Forest is cleared to get land for farming and industry. Some trees are also chopped down so their wood can be used for fuel, paper, furniture, or other products. Like all plants, trees soak up **carbon dioxide**, which they use to make food. Forest loss means that there are fewer trees to absorb carbon dioxide. On top of that, burning trees also releases carbon dioxide!

Farming

Lots of farmers spray their crops with human-made **fertilizers** that give the plants nitrogen so they grow well. Yet, when tiny living things in soil feed on the extra nitrogen, they release the **greenhouse gas nitrous oxide**. In addition, when cows and other farm animals burp and poop, they release the gas **methane**, which they make as they digest food!

Construction

Most homes, offices, bridges, and tunnels contain cement or concrete. These strong materials are made by baking limestone, clay, and other materials. Carbon dioxide is given off by the fuel used for heating as well as by the mixture as it bakes.

Fossil fuels

When we burn fossil fuels in factories, homes, and vehicles, we release carbon dioxide. Just as big a problem are **power plants,** where fossil fuels are burned to heat water to make steam, which flows through wheels called **turbines.** The spinning turbines are linked to **generators,** which turn the movement energy into electrical energy.

FUN FACT!

Every year, each large cow releases 265 lb (120 kg) of methane into the atmosphere.

Excuse me!

Extra greenhouse gases are trapping extra heat in the **atmosphere.** Right now, **emissions** of greenhouse gases are getting bigger, which is making Earth warm up faster. If emissions keep rising as fast as they are now, by the end of the century, Earth might be 9 °F (5 °C) warmer than it was in 1880. But if we really cut back on greenhouse gas emissions, scientists hope that Earth will be only 2.7 to 3.6 °F (1.5 to 2 °C) warmer.

THINK ABOUT IT!

In some regions, there is not enough farmland, so farmers clear forest to plant crops that will feed their family. Is it fair to tell them to stop doing it?

Precious ice

Ice is fun for skating and sliding, but it's super important in many other ways, too! In this chapter, let's find out more about our planet's precious ice. We'll also discover how much ice has melted so far.

The North and South **Poles** are covered by ice year-round. But why are our planet's poles colder than its **equator?** The sun shines more or less overhead at the equator. Yet, at the poles, the sun's rays hit Earth at an angle, giving much less warmth. Ice also covers the peaks of high mountains, because higher air is colder. When the air is cold, snow falls from clouds—not rain!

At 19,341 ft (5,895 m) high, the peak of Mount Kilimanjaro in Africa's Tanzania is covered by **glaciers,** even though it is almost on the equator. But around 85 percent of Kilimanjaro's ice melted between 1912 and 2011.

But it's so hot down here ...

Sheets of ice form when new snowfalls bury old snowfalls, pressing the old snow into ice. Different areas of ice have different names. "**Ice caps**" often means the ice covering the poles, but can also mean any big area of ice.

"**Glaciers**" are smaller areas of ice that are found on mountainsides and are often part of a larger **ice sheet.** Glaciers slide downhill, usually by around 10 in (25 cm) every day. "**Ice shelves**" are floating platforms of ice that form where a glacier meets the ocean. Finally, "**sea ice**" forms when sea water freezes, then floats on the sea surface.

Ice covers most of the island of Greenland, in the **Arctic** Ocean. Around 660,000 sq miles (1.7 million sq km) and up to 1.9 miles (3 km) thick, it's Earth's second largest body of ice, after the Antarctic ice cap.

DID YOU KNOW?

Around 12 percent of Earth's surface is currently covered by ice.

THINK ABOUT IT!

It's so cold on **Antarctica** that very few animals and no people live there all year round. Does that mean that Antarctica is unimportant?

Who says I'm not important?

PRECIOUS ICE

All sheets of ice melt at their edges, but—unless temperatures are rising—the lost ice is mostly replaced by new snowfall. Here's the problem: **Global warming** is making the **ice caps** melt faster than snow is falling. That's why they're shrinking!

Let's get serious about numbers for a moment ... Since the start of this century, the Antarctic ice cap has lost around 165 billion tons (150 billion metric tons) of ice every year. That's the amount of melted ice not replaced by new snow. The Greenland ice cap has lost 298 billion tons (270 billion metric tons) every year. It's easier to imagine these quantities if you know that a big walrus weighs around 1 ton!

DID YOU KNOW?
Earth is losing 1.3 trillion tons (1.2 trillion metric tons) of ice every year.

1 TON

Antarctica's ice shelves crumble into **icebergs** as they're warmed by sea and air.

Oh dear...

The **Arctic sea ice** has always melted partly during summer, shrinking to its smallest size by September. In September 1979, the sea ice covered 2.7 million sq miles (6.9 million sq km). But by September 2022, it covered only 1.8 million sq miles (4.7 million sq km). That's a lot less ice for walruses!

THINK ABOUT IT!

It can be difficult to understand problems we can't see for ourselves. Not many people have seen polar ice with their own eyes. Do you think that's why more people aren't taking action about global warming?

If I can't see it...

PRECIOUS ICE

Are the shrinking **ice caps** making life difficult for the animals that live on and around them? Let's focus on two very famous polar animals: the polar bear and the emperor penguin. That's one animal from each **pole!**

Polar bears spend most of their time on the **Arctic sea ice.** That's where they hunt for seals that are resting or have come up for air at holes in the ice. As the sea ice shrinks, some polar bears need to swim farther between patches of ice, which makes them tired and hungry. Now that ice is melting earlier in the year, many bears are also spending more time on land, where energy-rich food is hard to find.

The weight of the average Canadian polar bear has dropped by 15 percent in the last 20 years.

"Pick yourself up, Percy. No one noticed."

At the opposite pole, emperor penguins are at risk from the melting of sea ice around **Antarctica.** These birds nest on sea ice, then dive in the water to hunt tiny creatures called krill. Yet the number of krill is falling because young krill feed on plant-like **algae** that grow on sea ice. This means that emperor penguins are suffering from both loss of food and loss of **habitat!**

If sea ice continues to shrink at the current rate, by the end of this century the number of emperor penguins may have dropped by 80 percent.

FUN FACT!

Emperors are the largest penguins. They grow up to 3.9 ft (1.2 m) tall.

THINK ABOUT IT!

Which is your favorite polar animal? How would you feel if it became **extinct?**

1ST PRIZE

"Am I your favorite?"

17

In every **habitat**, animals—including humans—rely on each other for food. Changes in a habitat that harm one animal can make problems for others. Here are just some of the ways that melting **Arctic sea ice** is affecting local animals and people.

Arctic sea ice is shrinking, thinning, and melting earlier in the year.

With less sea ice to grow on, there is less **algae**, which means there's less food for small ocean creatures, which means less food for fish.

With less sea ice to be a lid on the Arctic Ocean, waves are growing larger and quickly eroding—or wearing away—the coasts. For example, the north coast of Alaska is moving inland by 4.6 ft (1.4 m) every year, destroying coastal homes, roads, and businesses.

Ocean-living mammals, such as seals and walruses, are losing the ice where they rest and mate. Seals are finding fewer fish to eat.

I've heard things are no better at the other **pole**.

Polar bears are losing their hunting grounds and finding fewer seals, leading to hunger and exhaustion for some.

Local peoples, such as the Inuit and Yupik of Alaska, Canada, Greenland, and Russia, can't travel safely across sea ice to reach family and friends. Traditional hunters are finding fewer seals and fish.

Polar bears are spending longer on land, where they are becoming more of a danger as they search for food in human towns.

Arctic foxes often follow polar bears across the sea ice to eat the remains of their kills, but with polar bears finding fewer seals, there is less food for foxes. Instead, Arctic foxes are more often eaten by desperate polar bears.

I'm following you.

No, I'm following YOU.

Meltdown!

How much more are the **ice caps** going to melt? Could they melt completely? And what effects will losing ice have on Earth? Read on to find out!

When scientists predict how much ice we'll lose, they talk about best-case and worst-case **scenarios**. A scenario is a series of events and outcomes.

To reach the best-case scenario, **greenhouse gas emissions** must be cut to nearly zero by 2050. If we did that, Earth would get no more than 2.7 to 3.6 °F (1.5 to 2 °C) warmer than in 1880. Even with this small rise, by 2050 the **Arctic** Ocean might have no ice during the hottest summers. But the good news is that the Antarctic and Greenland ice caps would not suffer big collapses.

DID YOU KNOW?

Even the best-case scenario would completely melt smaller mountain **glaciers**, such as Italy's Marmolada Glacier, by 2050.

"I'm not liking the worst-case scenario."

We would face the worst-case scenario if we let greenhouse gas emissions continue rising as quickly as now. By 2100, Earth's temperature might be 9 °F (5 °C) warmer than in 1880. By that year, the Arctic Ocean could be ice-free in summer and winter. Chunks of the Greenland and western Antarctic **ice sheet** could collapse.

But don't panic: These ice caps would take many thousands of years to melt completely!

The western Antarctic ice cap is more at risk than the east, because it ends in vast **ice shelves** that can be melted by seawater, which is warmer than the arctic air.

THINK ABOUT IT!

Do you think we'll face the worst-case scenario? Or do you think we'll make the changes we need to make?

MELTDOWN!

Melting ice causes rising **sea levels,** because the water flows into the oceans! On top of that, as **global warming** makes the oceans hotter, they expand a little—because warmer water takes up more room than colder water. This makes sea levels rise even more!

Let's start by looking at the numbers. Since 1880, the ocean has risen up the shore by 8 to 9 in (21 to 24 cm). Even our best-case **scenario** will see the ocean rise a further 1 to 2 ft (30 to 60 cm) by 2100. The very worst-case scenario would make sea levels rise up to 5.2 ft (1.6 m) by 2100—and a whopping 32.8 ft (10 m) by 2300!

A mix of rising sea levels and heavy rain causes floods in Thailand's coastal capital city, Bangkok.

A key cause of rising sea levels is melting land ice. Melting **sea ice** is not changing sea levels, because lots of that ice was already below the ocean surface. But melting **ice shelves** do raise sea level, because they're barriers that stop the movement of land ice into the sea.

As sea levels rise, low land by the coast will be flooded. This will affect the animals and plants that live by the sea. And what about humans? The humans most directly affected will be those living along coasts and on low-lying islands.

Let's discover more about the effects of **sea level** rise by focusing on the world's lowest country. The Maldives is a country of around 565,000 people who live on about 200 islands in the Indian Ocean. The islands have an average height above current sea level of 4.9 ft (1.5 m), and the highest land is just 7.9 ft (2.4 m).

The world takes strong action on **global warming**, so the sea floods only the Maldives' lowest coastal land by 2100.

During storms, high waves become more dangerous, forcing people to evacuate their homes. Fewer tourists visit the islands, so jobs are lost in the Maldives' many hotels.

Salty seawater soaks into underground sources of fresh water, leaving the islands short of drinking water.

Low-lying homes, businesses, and places of worship are lost.

THINK ABOUT IT!

If your family had to move away from your home town or village, what would you miss most?

I'm going to miss you...

WELCOME TO HOMEVILLE

Some Maldivians leave their homeland in search of safer homes and jobs.

The Maldivians protect themselves by building walls around islands and by pumping sand from the seafloor to make the ground higher. They also build new, higher islands. Work on all these projects has already begun. In 1997, construction started on the island of Hulhumalé, now home to 50,000 people. Work is also starting on a floating city with 5,000 homes.

The world takes little action on global warming, so sea-level rise makes most of the Maldives' islands **uninhabitable** by 2100.

A wall has been built around Malé, capital city of the Maldives.

The Maldivians have to abandon their homeland, perhaps moving to high land that their government is considering buying in India, Sri Lanka, or Australia. Far from home, the Maldivians must find new jobs and try to keep alive their language and traditions.

Animals found only in the Maldives—such as the Maldives sand wasp and Maldives damselfly—become **extinct**.

I'm buzzzzzing off...

MELTDOWN!

Unfortunately, rising **sea levels** will not be the only result of melting ice! As **meltwater** flows into the oceans around the Greenland and Antarctic **ice caps,** ocean **currents** could change. But what are currents anyway?

Currents are huge movements of water through the oceans. They are partly driven by the fact that cold water sinks and warm water rises because it's less dense (or less "heavy"). So what's the problem? Cold fresh water from melting ice caps could slow down currents, since fresh water is less dense than seawater and sinks more slowly.

It's nice to get the big picture.

Currents move warm water, heated around **the equator,** across the ocean surface toward **the poles.** Here it cools, sinks, and flows back toward the equator.

THINK ABOUT IT!

Can you name any jobs that are at risk from **climate change?** Read the information on the previous page, this page, and the next page for some ideas.

Some scientists think that even the best-case **scenario** would melt the Greenland ice cap enough to slow down currents in the North Atlantic Ocean. Despite **global warming,** this could cool down northwestern Europe because it would get less warming water.

Doesn't global warming make everywhere hotter?

DID YOU KNOW?

If the North Atlantic currents stopped completely, Britain's winter temperatures might cool by 9 to 18 °F (5 to 10 °C).

When ocean creatures die, they sink to the seafloor and break down into **nutrients.** Rising ocean currents carry these nutrients to the surface, where most sea creatures live. The nutrients are food for tiny creatures that are eaten by fish. If currents slow, fish will be affected, which will be a problem for people who make a living by catching fish.

MELTDOWN!

Do you know where the water in your faucet comes from? Millions of people get their drinking water from the partial melting of **glaciers** during spring and summer. The glacier **meltwater** flows downhill in streams and rivers. When snow falls in winter, it renews this water supply for another year.

So you want me to melt, but not too much?

The city of La Paz in Bolivia, South America, gets 30 percent of its water from glaciers.

If **global warming** completely melts many of the glaciers in a region, there will be lots of extra meltwater right away—perhaps enough to cause dangerous floods! Yet, in the years that follow, there will not be enough water for people and their animals and crops.

FUN FACT!

There are around 200,000 glaciers on the world's mountains and volcanoes.

28

Glacier meltwater also supplies electricity to millions of people. At the Three Gorges Dam, China, the Yangtze River turns **turbines,** which power electricity **generators.**

In Central Asia, the Himalaya, Karakoram, and Hindu Kush mountains are crowned by 55,000 glaciers. Almost 2 billion people live around the rivers that are supplied with water by these glaciers. The rivers include the 10 biggest in Asia, among them the Ganges, which runs through India and Bangladesh, and the Yangtze, which flows through China. Scientists think that—unless we keep temperature rise to less than 2.7 °F (1.5 °C)—up to two-thirds of the ice in the Central Asian mountains will be gone by 2100.

Hi! I'm Deliang Chen and I'm a Chinese Swedish **climate** scientist. I study how rising temperatures in Central Asia are affecting the region's water supply. I'm worried by how water loss will affect farmers, animals, and the landscape. Let's take action now!

MELTDOWN!

Here's some more news that's not so great! Melting of the **ice caps** could actually make **global warming** and **climate change** worse. When the results of a problem make the problem worse, it's known as a feedback.

The ice caps keep Earth cooler that it would be without them. Since ice is white and smooth—a little like a mirror—it reflects some of the sun's heat back into space. When ice melts, it exposes more dark ocean and rock to sunlight. Dark surfaces heat up easily, causing even warmer air and oceans, particularly at the **poles**. But this problem heats the whole planet a little more ...

Rising temperatures are already causing more periods of intensely hot weather, known as **heatwaves**. Melting ice caps could result in even more heatwaves, yet—strangely—melting ice could also cause more extremely cold weather in some regions ...

DID YOU KNOW?

In 2022, a record-breaking heatwave in China reached 104 °F (40 °C) and cost over $7 billion in lost crops and products.

Water!

Its melting **sea ice** is making the **Arctic** warm twice as fast as the rest of the planet! This is reducing the temperature difference between the North Pole and regions to the south. And that is weakening the polar jet stream, a fast wind that blows between the cold polar air and milder southern air. As the jet stream weakens, it often loops farther south, bringing freezing air with it.

The weakened jet stream brought freezing winters and heavy snow to North America and northern Europe in 2009–10, 2010–11, and 2013–14.

THINK ABOUT IT!

Some farmers are facing both more heatwaves and more freezing winters. How do you think this is affecting them?

What would happen in the worst-case scenario?

By 2100, a worst-case temperature rise of 9 °F (5 °C) has melted around 40 percent of Earth's ice. Large parts of the Antarctic and Greenland **ice caps** have collapsed. The **Arctic** Ocean is ice free. Around 80 percent of **glaciers** are gone.

Loss of their **habitat** drives some polar and mountain animals toward extinction.

Millions of people who rely on glacier **meltwater** lose their supplies of water and electricity, forcing them to abandon their homes and jobs.

Sea levels rise by up to 5.2 ft (1.6 m).

More dark rock and ocean are exposed, so less of the sun's heat is reflected back into space.

Changing ocean **currents** reduce the number of ocean fish, causing people who fish to move inland.

Millions of people living on low islands and coasts have to abandon their homes and jobs.

Warming air over the Arctic causes the melting of permafrost, the permanently frozen soil found in far northern parts of North America, Europe, and Asia. As the soil melts, tiny living things consume the once-frozen dead plants it contains, then release the **greenhouse gas methane** as they digest.

THINK ABOUT IT!

Do you live on low land near the sea? If you did, do you think you would be more worried about rising sea levels?

Climate change is worsened, leading to more extreme weather events that endanger people, animals, and crops.

Global warming is worsened, making the ice caps melt faster.

Hundreds of millions of people move to areas above sea level with sources of drinking water, increasing the need for land, water, homes, and jobs in those areas.

Farmers can grow less food, so the cost of food rises and some people go hungry.

Halt the melt

There's still time to save the **ice caps!** We can escape the worst-case **scenario** described on the previous page. In this chapter, let's look at the ways we can limit **global warming** and prevent its worst effects.

First, let's look at international efforts to slow global warming. Since 2015, more than 220 countries have signed on to the Paris Agreement, a promise to cut **greenhouse gas emissions.** This agreement aims to keep temperature rise to less than 3.6 °F (2 °C) and hopefully under 2.7 °F (1.5 °C), which would result in our best-case scenario of ice melt.

Officials celebrate the signing of the Paris Agreement by planting a tree!

The agreement sets out that each country will cut its greenhouse gas emissions by cutting the use of **fossil fuels** and stopping **deforestation.** It also agrees that money must be spent on protecting people, animals, and plants from **climate change** and **sea level** rise.

Let's examine some of the ways that governments and businesses are already cutting **greenhouse gas emissions.** But all of us can help stop the melt by making changes!

Problem: Burning oil in vehicle engines

Solutions: Businesses are investing in other ways to power vehicles, including electricity, sugar cane fuel, and hydrogen gas. We can all help if we make fewer car trips by taking the bus, walking, or bicycling.

Problem: Cutting down trees

Solutions: Governments, businesses, and charities are protecting our forests and planting trees. New projects are creating other jobs for loggers. You can help by buying paper products from managed forests, where at least one tree is planted for every tree felled.

Problem: Burning **fossil fuels** to make electricity

Solutions: Other sources of energy are being harnessed, including sunlight (which is turned into electricity by solar panels) and the wind, rivers, and oceans (which turn **turbines** to make electricity). Everyone can help by turning off electric appliances when they're not needed.

Problem: Releasing greenhouse gases from farms

Solutions: Governments are supporting farmers to cut their use of **fertilizers** and to give animals **methane**-reducing foods. All of us can try to waste less food and to eat less meat.

Growing me emitted 1 g of **carbon dioxide**, so eat me!

Problem: Using concrete and cement in construction

Solutions: Construction businesses are switching to recycled materials and to concrete made from alternatives, such as plants. New laws encourage the building of highly insulated homes that lose less heat in winter and get less hot in summer, which helps us use less fuel to stay warm or cool!

When I grow up, I'd like to be an apartment building.

FUN FACT!

In 1997, Costa Rica started paying farmers to protect forests—resulting in the size of the country's forests almost doubling since then!

THINK ABOUT IT!

Whose responsibility is it to fix **global warming**? Do you think it's governments, businesspeople, or farmers? Or do we all share responsibility?

HALT THE MELT

As we've found out, there's no way to keep our precious **ice caps** from melting a little more! So, while we work to slow that melt, we also need to protect ourselves—and other animals—from rising **sea levels** and loss of ice.

Across the world, coastal towns and villages are being protected from rising sea levels by the building of such barriers as seawalls. Where beaches, mangrove forests, and marshes are being flooded, **conservationists** are helping these **habitats** move inland, by buying coastal land and preventing construction.

The low-lying city of Rotterdam, in the Netherlands, is protecting itself from rising sea levels by building floating homes.

Volunteers are planting seedlings to extend a coastal marsh. These marshes are home to crabs and wading birds. They also protect inland areas from flooding by soaking up water during high tides and storms.

Polar animals are the species most directly at risk from melting ice caps. Conservationists are helping them by also fighting all the other threats to their survival. For example, polar bears also face danger from pollution, shipping, mining, and tourism. Conservationists remind everyone about bears' needs while campaigning for new laws to protect them.

Hi! I'm the Omani scientist Rumaitha al Busaidi. I'm worried by how rising sea levels are making saltwater seep into freshwater wells in coastal Oman. Most plants can't cope with saltwater, so farmers can't water their crops unless it rains. I'm helping coastal farmers set up fish farms instead, where fish are bred, fed, and caught in large pools.

THINK ABOUT IT!

Can you think of any changes you could make to cut down your **greenhouse gas emissions?** Take a look at the previous page for some ideas.

No! Just leave your car at home and bicycle instead!

Conclusion

Humans have made a mistake! While we've been trying to travel faster and build higher, we forgot to take care of our planet. And so, the **ice caps** are smaller today than they were yesterday. But it's not too late to slow the melt, so there will be ice caps for thousands of tomorrows.

If we work together to cut **greenhouse gas emissions,** we can keep Earth from getting more than 2.7 to 3.6 °F (1.5 to 2 °C) hotter than it was in 1880. This would save the ice caps from major melting. And that would stop **sea level** rise and **climate change** from endangering millions of homes, jobs, and lives.

Many countries have already cut their greenhouse gas emissions and are working hard to cut them more. For example, the 27 countries of the European Union have reduced their emissions by more than a quarter since 1990.

For you and me, it's difficult to make changes to how we travel, eat, and buy. Yet, over the last few years, we've gained new heroes—such as Swedish **climate** campaigner Greta Thunberg—who set us an example. They remind us that, if we care about the ice caps, we can play our part in saving them!

From the age of 15, Greta Thunberg has told the world that we must stop **global warming.**

FUN FACT!

The use of wind **turbines** instead of fossil-fuel **power plants** is cutting the world's greenhouse gas emissions by 1.3 billion tons (1.2 billion metric tons) every year.

China has more wind turbines than any other country, supplying 7 percent of its power.

THINK ABOUT IT!

Has anyone you've read about in this book inspired you to save the ice caps?

Summary

Will the **ice caps** melt so fast they cause catastrophe? Check your understanding of the possibilities described in this book.

Greenhouse gases are released by vehicles, factories, and **power plants,** as well as by logging, farming, and construction.

By 2100, Earth's temperature is no more than 2.7 to 3.6 °F (1.5 to 2 °C) warmer than in 1880.

The **Arctic sea ice** disappears in hot summers, small **glaciers** melt, and some Antarctic and Greenland ice shelves crumble.

Extra greenhouse gases in the **atmosphere** trap the sun's heat, making Earth around 1.9 °F (1 °C) hotter today than in 1880.

Greenhouse gas **emissions** are cut to nearly zero by 2050.

The Arctic sea ice disappears, most glaciers melt, and large parts of the Greenland and Antarctic ice caps collapse.

Greenhouse gas emissions continue to rise.

By 2100, Earth's temperature is around 9 °F (5 °C) warmer than in 1880.

42

By 2100, **sea levels** rise by 1 to 2 ft (30 to 60 cm).

People living on low coasts need help to protect their homes, farms, and freshwater sources.

THINK ABOUT IT!

In a hundred years' time, will children wonder why we did so little about the melting ice caps? Or do you think we'll make the right choices—and future children will be grateful to us?

Polar and coastal animals need help as they lose their **habitat** and food.

Ice melt worsens **global warming,** changes ocean **currents** and winds, and—as warm water evaporates from the oceans—puts more water in the atmosphere.

Extra heat and water in the atmosphere cause dangerous storms, while blizzards and **heatwaves** put lives and crops at risk.

By 2100, sea levels rise by up to 5.2 ft (1.6 m).

Hundreds of millions of people leave coasts and regions that rely on glacier **meltwater** for drinking.

Billions of people face shortages of food, water, homes, and jobs.

Glossary

algae—plantlike living things that usually grow in water

Antarctica—the large area of land around the South Pole

Arctic—the region, mostly covered by ocean, around the North Pole

atmosphere—the blanket of gases that surrounds Earth, including nitrogen and oxygen, plus smaller amounts of such gases as carbon dioxide

carbon dioxide—a greenhouse gas that's found naturally in the atmosphere and is also released by burning fossil fuels or trees

climate—the usual weather in a region, such as cold and rainy

climate change—changes in the world's weather—in particular, an increase in extreme weather—that are mainly due to human activity

conservationist—a person who works to protect habitats and animals

current—a large, riverlike movement of water through the ocean

deforestation—the loss of forests due to clearing land for farming or factories

emission—a release, such as giving off gas

equator—an imaginary line around Earth's middle, halfway between the North and South poles

extinct—an extinct animal or plant no longer exists because its entire species has died out, just like the dinosaurs

fertilizer—a material that's put on fields to make plants grow well

fossil fuel—a fuel, such as natural gas, oil, or coal, which was formed over millions of years from the remains of animals and plants

generator—a machine that turns movement, such as the spinning of a turbine, into electricity

glacier—an area of ice that forms on mountains

global warming—an increase in temperatures on Earth due to the greenhouse effect

greenhouse effect—the way that some gases in the atmosphere—including carbon dioxide, methane, and nitrous oxide—trap the sun's heat

greenhouse gas—a gas that traps heat in the atmosphere

habitat—the place where an animal or plant usually lives

heatwave—days or weeks of extremely hot weather

iceberg—a floating chunk of ice that broke off a glacier or ice sheet

ice cap—the ice covering the poles—or any large area of ice

ice sheet—a huge area of ice

ice shelf—a platform of ice that forms where a glacier meets the sea

meltwater—water formed by melting snow or ice

methane—a greenhouse gas that's found in "natural gas" fuel and is also released by burping and farting farm animals

nitrous oxide—a greenhouse gas that's released from fertilized soil

nutrient—something living things need in order to grow

pole—Earth's most northerly point or most southerly point

power plant—a factory that makes electricity

scenario—an imagined series of events

sea ice—ice that forms on very cold seawater

sea level—the height of the ocean's surface

turbine—a machine for making electricity with a wheel that's turned by flowing air, steam, or water

uninhabitable—impossible to live in

45

Review and reflect

COMPREHENSION QUESTIONS

Getting hotter
- If Earth's climate has been far hotter and far colder than it is now, why is it problematic that we are experiencing global warming today?
- What is the greenhouse effect and why is it problematic?

Precious ice
- Where can ice be found on Earth? Why is this?
- How does looking at the cause and effect diagram on pages 18 and 19 help you understand how changes in one habitat that harm one living thing can make problems for others?

Meltdown!
- What will happen if ice shelves melt and cause the sea level to rise slightly?
- Of all the possible effects of the ice caps melting, which most inspires you to want to stop the melt? Why?

Halt the melt
- In 2015, more than 220 countries signed the Paris Agreement. What does this agreement include?
- What is inspiring or hopeful about American scientist Susan Solomon's work around chlorofluorocarbons in the late 1980's?

Conclusion and summary
- After reading this book and considering what would happen if the ice caps melt, what is your biggest takeaway? Why?

MAKE A CHAIN OF EVENTS!

Creating a paper chain can help you explore and visualize how cause and effect relationships can be thought of as a sequence of events.

You'll need:
- Pencil
- Scratch paper
- Pens or markers
- Stapler and staples
- Strips of paper (2 colors, if possible)

Instructions:

1. **Select a focus:** Choose a specific aspect from the book that caught your attention—it could be something that has increased global warming and led to climate change, or something that would happen (or is already happening!) due to the ice caps melting.

2. **Brainstorm causes and effects:** On a sheet of scratch paper, brainstorm and list the causes and effects related to your chosen focus. Think critically about the factors that contributed to or resulted from your focus. You can always look back in the text for ideas!

3. **Write on strips:** Write each cause and each effect on its own strip of paper. If you have different colored paper, use one color for the cause strips and the other for the effect strips.

4. **Create the paper chain:** Organize your strips into causes and effects. Start forming a paper chain to show how a cause leads to an effect. Use the stapler to connect the two strips. Continue adding cause and effect strips as links in your chain. When you've finished, you should be able to start at the beginning of your chain and read through each chain link in a logical order.

5. **Linking multiple chains:** If your focus has multiple causes or effects, you can create additional chains and link them together to show how complex cause and effect relationships can be!

Write about it!

Look at the paper chain you created and how the causes link to effects (which in turn link to other causes!). How might breaking a link in the chain impact the overall sequence of events?

World Book, Inc.
180 North LaSalle Street
Suite 900
Chicago, Illinois 60601
USA

For information about other World Book publications, visit our website at www.worldbook.com or call 1-800-WORLDBK (967-5325).

For information about sales to schools and libraries, call 1-800-975-3250 (United States), or 1-800-837-5365 (Canada).

© 2024 (print and e-book) by World Book, Inc. All rights reserved. No part of this publication may be reproduced, stored in a retrieval system, or transmitted in any form or by any means (electronic, mechanical, photocopying, recording, or otherwise) without written permission from World Book, Inc.

WORLD BOOK and the GLOBE DEVICE are registered trademarks or trademarks of World Book, Inc.

Library of Congress Cataloging-in-Publication Data for this volume has been applied for.

What Would Happen If...?
978-0-7166-5448-3 (set, hc.)

The Ice Caps Melted?
ISBN: 978-0-7166-5452-0 (hc.)

Also available as:

ISBN: 978-0-7166-5458-2 (e-book)
ISBN: 978-0-7166-5464-3 (soft cover)

Staff

Editorial

Vice President
Tom Evans

Editorial Project Coordinator
Kaile Kilner

Curriculum Designer
Caroline Davidson

Proofreader
Nathalie Strassheim

Graphics and Design

Senior Visual Communications Designer
Melanie Bender

Digital Asset Specialist
Rosalia Bledsoe

Written by Claudia Martin
Illustrated by Paula Bossio

Developed with World Book by
White-Thomson Publishing LTD
www.wtpub.co.uk

Acknowledgments

4-5	© Risto Raunio, Shutterstock; © Max Dallocco, Shutterstock
6-7	© Daniel Eskridge, Shutterstock; Ittiz (licensed under CC BY-SA 3.0 DEED)
8-9	© Maximillian cabinet/Shutterstock; © Alexander Knyazhinsky, Shutterstock; © Artur Nyk, Shutterstock
10-11	© Rich Carey, Shutterstock; © Fotokostic/Shutterstock; © ETAJOE/Shutterstock; © Rudmer Zwerver, Shutterstock
12-13	© Volodymyr Burdiak, Shutterstock; © Vadim_N/Shutterstock
14-15	© M. Unal Ozmen, Shutterstock; © Louie Lea, Shutterstock; © Hekla/Shutterstock
16-17	© sirtravelalot/Shutterstock; © Ondrej Prosicky, Shutterstock
20-21	© Gaearon Tolon, Shutterstock; © Epic Vision/Shutterstock
22-23	© Wutthichai/Shutterstock; © Marius Dobilas, Shutterstock
24-25	© Shevchenko Andrey, Shutterstock; © Chumash Maxim, Shutterstock; © Altug Galip, Shutterstock
26-27	© Kitnha/Shutterstock; © Sampajano Anizza, Shutterstock; © Hekla/Shutterstock
28-29	© Isabel Kendzior, Shutterstock; © javarman/Shutterstock
30-31	© Siegi/Shutterstock
34-35	© a katz/Shutterstock; © Namomooyim/Shutterstock
36-37	© esbobeldijk/Shutterstock; © Teo Tarras, Shutterstock
38-39	© Edwin Muller Photography/Shutterstock; © Cavan Images/Alamy Images
40-41	© maple90/Shutterstock; © Mauro Ujetto, Shutterstock
45	© Wutthichai/Shutterstock
46-47	© Roi and Roi/Shutterstock

www.ingramcontent.com/pod-product-compliance
Lightning Source LLC
Chambersburg PA
CBHW060944170426
43197CB00023B/2977